- A better communicator
- More influential
- Able to brief people more clearly
- Aware of how to write for your audience
- More likely to achieve your goals

KU-685-930

Focusing your message

Today we will explore some of the basics and build our understanding of what will make your writing more appealing and effective. Remember that people rarely seek out business copy to read. To be successful, business writing has to capture people's attention, then make them act on the messages it conveys.

Today, you will:

- Understand why you must focus on results
- Discover how to structure any piece of writing
- Learn some important terms and what they mean
- Look at the words guaranteed to 'hook' your reader

Focus on the result

Before starting to write your copy, jot down what you want to happen as a result of your words being read. Try to prioritise them as follows:

As a result of reading my copy my audience will:
- **Know** the facts that I want to communicate
- **Think** that my idea/offer is worth considering
- **Do** something to let me know they have understood

For example, in a memo that asks people to attend a meeting, you want them to:

Copywriting
in a week

ROBERT ASHTON

Hodder & Stoughton

A MEMBER OF THE HODDER HEADLINE GROUP

Orders: please contact Bookpoint Ltd, 130 Milton Park, Abingdon, Oxon
OX14 4SB.
Telephone: (44) 01235 827720. Fax: (44) 01235 400454. Lines are open from
9.00–6.00, Monday to Saturday, with a 24 hour message answering service.
Email address: orders@bookpoint.co.uk

British Library Cataloguing in Publication Data
A catalogue record for this title is available from The British Library

ISBN 0 340 81194 3

First published   2003
Impression number   10 9 8 7 6 5 4 3 2 1
Year   2007 2006 2005 2004 2003

Typeset by SX Composing DTP, Rayleigh, Essex.
Printed in Great Britain for Hodder & Stoughton Educational, a division of
Hodder Headline Plc, 338 Euston Road, London NW1 3BH by
Cox & Wyman Ltd, Reading, Berkshire.

■■■C O N T E N T S■■■

For millennia, people have communicated in writing. The written word can influence large numbers of people and can be read at any time, not just when you are there to speak to them. What is more, writing things down enables people to think, plan and edit, which cannot be done in an off-the-cuff speech.

Although you are already literate, in a business context you must do much more than just tell the story. Here, words have to work making the reader think or act differently and delivering the payback the writer is seeking.

Reading this book and practising the techniques it introduces will make you a more effective writer. Expertise in grammar is not necessary, as all the necessary terms are simply defined; in fact, some forms of business writing deliberately flout the rules. This book is for the people who want to write for results.

Successful business writing makes you:

- **Know**: when and where the meeting is, how long it will take and what will be covered
- **Think**: about what they can contribute to the discussion, and that there will be a clear benefit to them if they attend
- **Do**: let you know if they can attend and if not, who can come in their place

If you need six people to turn up to represent at least five of the eight teams in your company, you know what a successful result looks like.

Next, think about some pressing goals that you need to achieve through others. Try to list the objectives in terms of what you want people to **know**, **think** and **do**. It would make focusing a lot easier. When you start writing, it will also make it a lot clearer for your reader. If your message is clear, people will be more likely to understand it.

Structure to succeed

Even if you never meet a customer, it could still be argued that your business copy is sales copy. This is because business writing has to be persuasive and, as we all know, sales copy is the most persuasive of all. Even our example above, in which we seek to arrange a meeting, has to persuade people to attend, people who no doubt have other things to do. When you write, you are substituting your words for your voice. If you are writing sales copy, your words are making a 'sales presentation' and need to follow the structure of a sales interview. Let's take a look at the stages of the sales process, as this provides a useful structure for almost any business writing situation. It can work well, even if all you are selling is the need to stand away from the edge of a cliff.

1 *Getting attention*: before your advertisement, poster, website, report or proposal gets read, it has to attract the eye of your target reader and compete with interesting editorial, proposals written by your rivals and much more besides. Later, we will cover techniques that can help you, but for now, focus on the need to make your introduction punchy, relevant, exciting and able to communicate the nub of your message in a split second.

2 *Make it personal*: you will be familiar with those cheesy mailshots that mention your name, address and something about you on every other line. These letters are written by experts. They know that using your name and referring to things you can relate to will make the letter personal to you. Face-to-face, reassuring personal messages are transmitted through body language. However, you will not be standing in front of your reader, so your words have to do this for you.

3 *Reasons to stay reading*: most people have a short attention span and are easily distracted; your writing has to hold their interest. This is best achieved using benefits. For example, we want you to keep reading this book because then you will become a better writer and will gain a healthy return on your investment. This is achieved by hinting at what is to follow in later chapters, which should help keep your interest and build your expectations. The back cover outlines what is inside and, once inside, you are

drip fed with hints that expand on those promised benefits. If you think back to the 'know, think, do' sequence, you can begin to see how you can introduce 'build up' to your writing, maintain interest and keep your reader with you.

4 *Overcoming likely objections*: you have grabbed attention, made it personal and added some relevant benefits. Your reader will now be looking for the catch. What you have to do is pre-empt their objection by providing the answer before the doubt pops into their head. Project proposals are a good example of where this is really important. A section that breaks down the budget and resource implications and spells out the return is a great way to allay fears. You have to put yourself in the shoes of your reader, imagine how they will react, and then make sure you include the answer. Of course they can always contact you to ask the question, but then you have lost the opportunity to get immediate commitment.

5 *Being believable*: even business writing is a creative medium and you can say almost anything if you have the skill and technique to make your argument look credible. Your reader may realise this, so your text has to be underpinned with fact, or at least testimonial. To avoid litigation, particularly with advertising and promotional copy, you have to be careful only to make honest claims that can be supported. Remember too that operating manuals, personnel documents and even warning signs can, if misleading, land you in trouble.

Consider the following statement:

In independent tasting trials most people preferred cola brand X. We think your customers will prefer it too.

As a shopkeeper, this might seem reason enough to stock brand X. Read it again. The independent trials were probably conducted in the street by a research company and there are ways to bias tasting trials (for example, the first product tasted is often preferred to the second). Secondly, the writer only *thinks* your customers will prefer brand X. If your customers hate it, you cannot sue the writer.

6 *Call to action*: this is the most important role of your business writing, for it delivers the result. Seek a realistic result: do not ask too much of your reader. It is also important to encourage a response you can measure. For example, if your letter invites the reader to log on to a business website, offer some incentive or set up a separate 'front page' for the promotion, so that you can relate resulting 'hits' to the letter and track success.

It is now time for you to write something that illustrates this sequence. Imagine that you are selling coach holidays and are writing a letter to encourage your customers to book early (to enable you to confirm your hotel bookings and boost your cash flow with their deposits). You have already sent out your new brochure and many of your regulars have booked. You feel that a well-written letter will encourage 100 more people who travelled with you last year to book again this year. You have a list, so each letter is mail merged to make it personal. It might read something like this (stages 1–6 are marked in):

Dear Mrs Smith

(1) DON'T MISS YOUR CHANCE TO TAKE THE PICK OF OUR HOLIDAYS FOR NEXT SUMMER!

(2) I know that you really enjoyed your holiday with us last year and am a little surprised that your booking was not amongst the many we have already received for next year. Some of our more popular destinations are already booking fast.

(3) As a regular customer, we would also like to reward your loyalty with a free welcome pack of speciality teas and biscuits (worth £10), which will be waiting in your hotel room if you book your holiday before the end of February.

(4) May I also remind you that we never discount our holidays at the last minute so there is no benefit in delaying your booking. This is because our holidays are carefully priced to be competitive with rival operators and because we are usually able to book our hotels ahead of others. We enjoy healthy discounts that enable us to offer you excellent value for money.

(5) I have enclosed a copy of an article in the Anytown Journal that compares our holidays with the major national coach tour companies. If you read it, you will see why we were so delighted when it was published; it is very flattering.

(6) Remember too that all you need to pay now is your £50 deposit to secure a place on the holiday of your choice. A booking form, reply-paid envelope and list of

holidays is enclosed. Please telephone me if you have any questions, otherwise I look forward to hearing from you soon.

Yours sincerely,

Fred Greengrass
Tour Manager

Now you have seen an example, think of a situation where you need to write a business letter to a customer and see if you can follow the one to six format. You will not necessarily have one sentence for each section: you may be able to include several sections in a single sentence. What is important is that all six are adequately covered.

Some useful terms

Many copywriting books are packed with technical terms,
which can make you feel unprepared and ignorant of the
finer points of English grammar, rather than encourage you
to experiment. This book makes no such demands on the
reader. However, there are a few writing techniques with
which you need to feel comfortable that have somewhat
daunting names. However, if you tackle them one at a time,
you will see that they add flavour and impact to your
writing. Business text can be dry, packed with information
and leave no time to savour the concepts the writer is trying
to communicate. Truly effective writing paints pictures in the
reader's mind and leaves just enough to the imagination to
make the reader think they drew the right conclusion on their
own. Some favourites are:

- *Metaphor*: a figure of speech in which one thing is
  described as something quite different: for example, '*All
  the world's a stage*'. Using metaphor enables you to inject
  subtle humour and, more importantly, to provide an
  opportunity for your reader's imagination to kick in. In a
  business context, describing an office as a 'hive of activity'
  is a metaphor: it implies that everyone is busy.

- *Simile*: this is where two essentially unlike things are
  deliciously compared with each other. This provides more
  opportunities for humour and fires the reader's
  imagination: for example, '*his desk was as cluttered as the bin
  outside a chip shop*'. '*His customers placed orders like free-
  falling lemings*'.

- *Alliteration*: commonly used in advertising headlines or in
  titles of proposals or reports, this is where a sequence of

words all start with the same letter. Alliterated lines catch the eye and are easily remembered. This technique can be used for the tackiest (*buy bumper basement bargains*) to the most subtle purpose (*does dental decay daunt dentists?*)

- *Enjambment*: a term used by poets to describe the way the word at the end of a line leaves you hanging, eager to discover what is revealed by the line below.

  It is useful when you are working with designers and need to determine where to put line breaks in a column of text. For example:

  'we know you will be delighted with what

  our range of lipsticks will do for your smile.'

- *Oxymoron*: this is the conjoining of two contradictory words which together say something rather special. They are often used to emphasise things you want your reader to know, think or do, for example *'Our children's Halloween masks are pretty ugly.'*

- *Homophones*: also used to emphasise key points. Homophones are words that sound the same but are spelled differently, such as son and sun. For example, *'you know our sauce comes from a reputable source.'* They make the reader stop and think.

You do not need to remember all these terms: just practise them and adopt those that suit your personal style and type of business. An estate agent will use different words in different ways from a travel agent. However, before you move on, try the following exercise. It will encourage you to experiment and push out the boundaries of your writing.

You will soon see which techniques you enjoy using and which irritate you. Why not try them all, and then focus on those you are most comfortable with? You can always add others later.

Imagine that you are managing a leisure centre. You have to write text that will influence the general public, but you also have to motivate your team and encourage them to follow good practice. Write some simple statements that might help explain this using:

- *Metaphor*: for a poster advertising swimming lessons
- *Simile*: for a memo encouraging gym staff to keep the equipment clean
- *Alliteration*: for the day's specials on the cafeteria blackboard
- *Enjambment*: on promotional T-shirts for a community 'fun run'
- *Oxymoron*: to describe the 'employee of the month'
- *Homophone*: for a 'keep fit' slogan

Do not worry if you find this quite challenging: it will get easier with practice. Remember that this is all about making your business writing more effective: ask others to give you honest feedback.

Hooking your reader

The best way to win over your reader is to flatter them. This is clearly easier if you have more information about them, for example for a letter to a small group. Here you can use the reader's name, or their organisation's name at least, to make the message personal.

With advertising, and to some extent with direct mail you will know little about your reader until they respond and identify themselves. In this situation, it is good to remember some basic social rules. We all like to be acknowledged, and the most powerful word you can use is 'you'. Use phrases such as, *'we know that you enjoy our barbecue sauce'*, which sounds much more appealing than *'our barbecue sauce is enjoyed by millions.'* The reader is not really interested in the majority view: they want it to taste nice to them.

Summary

Today you started your journey from literate individual to competent copywriter. You recognised the importance of clarity and focus in your writing, and practised planning exactly what you want your reader to know, think and do as a result of reading your words.

Then, you looked at the sequence in which information should be given. Your reader needs encouragement to start reading, to stay with you and then, ideally, to give you some measurable feedback.

Next, you were introduced to some terms that describe interesting ways in which you can arrange words to boost their effect. With practice you will naturally adopt some of these techniques and forget their technical names.

Lastly, you learnt the importance of making the message personal to your audience.

You will have a chance to cover some of these points again as you look in more detail at some different situations where your growing skills as a business copywriter can help you achieve more in your job.

Using layout, pictures and colour to make words memorable

Before you start writing, it is worthwhile spending some time considering how people read. Your reader will be influenced by the way in which you present your writing, as well as by the words that you use. You need to recognise the significance of shape, layout, illustrations and even the texture of your document.

Today, you will:

- Discover how the eye scans a page and what this means
- Understand the value of pictures and where to find them
- Consider some typographical techniques that help words 'stick'
- Learn what makes words, especially product names, memorable
- Appreciate why you should be explicit

How people read

You may assume that, in the West at least, our eye starts scanning the page from the top left hand corner. Indeed, as you reflect on your eye's journey to this point on the page, you may not realise that before starting to read the words, your eye quickly scanned the whole page before choosing where to begin. The cartoon, for example, will almost certainly have caught your eye and been viewed before you read a single word.

A lot of research has been carried out into the way that information transfers from the page to the reader's brain: in the advertising industry it is a science. You do not need to study too much of the theory, but as an effective copywriter, you should know the basics.

Imagine that your document, advertisement, or business card is divided into four equal quarters. X marks the spot that your eye will automatically go to first on the page. Experts call this the 'primary optical area'. The eye will then travel up towards the top left hand corner, then follow the Z shape as depicted below:

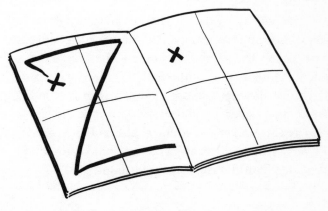

This visual flow, or eye-path, tells you where you have to position the most important, attention-grabbing thing you have. This will arouse the reader's interest and make them, without even realising it, slow down and look more closely at what you have prepared.

Look at some advertisements: this is where the phenomenon is most often exploited. Take a ruler and pencil and draw the Z shape over the top of the ad. Can you see how often the message builds as you follow the line of the Z? A picture usually covers at least the primary optical area and often more of the page. You are then led to the headline, which often starts with a distinctive letter, symbol of even a starburst to make the corner of the Z, and then feeds you the key benefit. The long diagonal takes you through the picture again and the detailed text, called 'body copy'. The Z ends with what is termed the 'call to action': a telephone number, coupon or shop address. We will cover this in more detail on Wednesday.

Using pictures

There is an old saying that 'a picture can save a thousand words': this is still true today. Although some people are more receptive to pictures than others, the simple fact is that people will look at the picture first, then read the words. It makes sense, therefore, to use pictures, diagrams and graphs wherever you can to get your point across, as they improve understanding and speed comprehension. There are few occasions when an illustration of some kind cannot add impact, weight and sense to your writing.

Another useful trick from advertising is that we like to see pictures of people: not surprising when you think that the first thing we learn to recognise as a baby is usually our mother's face. Conversely, adults are most affected by young-looking faces, which is why cartoon characters often have large heads in relation to their bodies. It makes the whole body seem baby-like, vulnerable and appealing and also places more emphasis on the facial expression.

Some useful points to consider when selecting pictures to illustrate your work are:

What	Why
One or many?	One large picture has more impact than several small ones
Colour or black	Colour is not a panacea: content is more important
People	Faces get noticed: men look at men, women at women. Use different people to illustrate inclusivity
Backgrounds	The best pictures are close-ups with no background
Oddities	A small oddity can catch attention, such as an eyepatch on a beautiful girl
Endorsement	Your van in front of Buckingham Palace will imply more than the same van photographed in a multi-storey car park

Finding good pictures

It is worth spending a moment thinking about where you can source good pictures to illustrate your writing.

Below are a few tips:

- Ask your customers and suppliers, where appropriate, to provide photographs
- Always carry a camera in your car to capture chance opportunities
- There are many online photo-libraries where you can download images
- Graphic designers usually have an eye for good pictures and can also draw for you
- You can buy 'royalty-free' CDs, packed with all kinds of pictures

And a few things to avoid:

- Do not use clip art unless you really have to: it is too widely used. Be different
- Do not infringe anyone's copyright or 'steal' images: you could end up in Court
- Wherever possible, get permission to publish someone's photo in advertisements
- Remember that some people are easily offended, so avoid controversial images

Graphs

Too often, you will see figures presented in columns and tables. Whilst this is preferable when presenting facts to an accountant, most people would prefer to see the data summarised in graphic form. Most commonly used spreadsheet packages can produce graphs for you. If figures form a major part of your business communication, consider developing your spreadsheet skills so that you are comfortable using the graphics and formulae. Graphs will enable your reader to grasp the key trends in a flash: position them where they will be seen first, so that they prepare the reader for the detailed information that follows them.

Colour

When you are producing printed documents, colour inevitably adds to the cost. With text, however, more colour does not necessarily mean more impact: if your work appears too kaleidoscopic, people will avoid it. Although most offices now have colour copiers and colour printers, you do not have to use all the features available to you.

Colour is best used to:

- Highlight key points, e.g. coloured text for a key passage in a lengthy tract
- Convey mood, e.g. red for aggressive, green for environmental, as a background
- Illustrate detail, e.g. in technical or scientific drawings and documents

However, experts have estimated that advertising responses can be up to 50% higher when colour is used instead of black and white. It depends on your message, your industry and your audience.

Before leaving pictures and shape to move on to words, you may find it helpful to do an exercise that will reinforce the points covered so far. Take a pile of magazines, newspapers and journals that are relevant to your favourite hobby. Using an A4 piece of paper, some scissors and glue, create a montage, using pictures only, that conveys a positive message about your chosen subject. Remember to use the 'Z' to position your pictures in a logical sequence and to use people as well as things. A good tip is to use faces to show feelings and things to inform: you might have a smiling face and a fast car. When you have finished, show the picture to someone you trust and see if they get the message.

Presenting words

Now that you understand how important illustrations are, it is time to get back to words. Words are, in effect, also viewed as pictures. When we read, we do not study each letter. Instead, we scan the line and use the shape of the whole word to identify it and translate it into an image or a perception in our mind.

The art of formatting text is called typography and, as with pictures, most of the research into this subject relates to advertising. As it could be argued that all business copywriting is advertising, since it seeks to 'sell' a concept, idea or product, it is appropriate to examine how good typography can give your writing a winning edge.

Fonts

For every written piece we create on our PC or have produced by a designer, we have a choice of typeface or font. Some are old and trusted, others new and stylish. Many organisations have a 'house font' in which all corporate communication must be set. This then becomes part of the organisation's brand, and manuals are produced that define how every document, printed leaflet and advertisement should look. Banks and insurance companies usually have such a system.

For you, it may be a question of personal taste and preference. Fonts fall into two main styles. Serifed fonts have letters with little tails, which bounce your eye from letter to letter and word to word. Serifed text is, in theory, easier to read than plain, 'san serif' text. On your PC you can usually choose a font such as 'Arial', which is san serif, or 'Times', which is serifed. Try composing some text in a number of different fonts of each type and see which you find easier to read.

Typographic tips

There are a number of easy-to-remember tips that can increase the legibility of the text that you create. Remember that your reader is not necessarily going to be someone you know. They may be older, younger, speak English as a second language or have poor eyesight. The more you can do to help them, the more likely they are to read what you have written. Below are some popular typographical tips:

- Starting a block of text with a 'drop capital', where the first letter is larger than the rest, increases readership.
- Keep sentences short, with no more than 16 words
- In letters and proposals, use 11 point type and 1.5 line spacing
- Use bold and italics to highlight key points; colour can also be used
- Widows (single words that have spilled over onto the next line) make text blocks less block-like and daunting to the reader. (Designers, however, do not like widows and try to remove them!)

Choosing words

Having looked at how words should be arranged, it is time to choose the words to use. You may yourself have a wide and varied vocabulary. What is more important, however, is the vocabulary range of your reader. If your writing is too simple, it can seem patronising; too complex and it will appear unapproachable or pretentious. You have to achieve a balance between the two and write words that your reader will understand.

It is also important not to repeat the same word too often, as this makes your writing boring to read and does little for your credibility. Buy yourself a good thesaurus and use it regularly to find commonly used alternatives for these words. You can also buy and download PC-based thesaurus packages, which enable you to highlight a word, explore alternatives and replace it with one your prefer. Less relevant, but fun all the same, are the websites that send you a new word every day (such as www.dictionary.com). Subscribing to these can broaden your general vocabulary, as well as brighten your day.

Making new words

In a marketing environment, the generation of new words to name products and services is an industry in itself. If you are a marketer, you will know that giving something new a name defines it, and makes it easier to focus on its benefits.

Some of the most memorable brand names, for example Kodak, are almost what are termed palindromes: they sound almost the same read backwards as forwards.

As an exercise, why not try to think of new names for products or services that your organisation produces. Remember that old products can be cheaply refreshed with revised names, new packaging and very few new features.

Be explicit

The more you beat around the bush, the more frustrated and anxious your reader will become. It is always better to be explicit and say exactly what you mean, then expand on the point in the following sentence. This is infinitely better than working up to the punch line. Below are a couple of examples:

> Using our detergent means you can reduce water temperature and save 20% on your fuel bills. This is because the product is packed with modified enzymes that are able to digest stains at a lower temperature.

> Kennel-X in your dog's bowl will make his tail wag faster. The specially formulated crunchy nuggets are tasty and keep teeth and gums healthy. A healthy dog is a happy dog.

In both examples, the key benefit message is contained in the first, short sentence. The words that follow expand on the message and justify the claim.

It is now time for you to write some explicit text. Go back to the montage you made earlier and write some copy about the message you were expressing. Make the first sentence explicit and then support it with two more that emphasise and illustrate the benefits you are seeking to convey. Remember the importance of using the word 'you' to make the message personal to the reader. Then put your words on screen and experiment with different fonts. Can you see how to bring it all together?

Summary

You have now explored the visual aspects of creative writing. You have a much better grasp of how people read and have practised ways in which you can make it easier for people to get your message. Pictures can say so much, but they do need supporting words to explain exactly what it is the picture is saying. In fact, it has been proven that captions under pictures are a good way of reinforcing advertising messages. Spend some time looking at how others present their writing and reflect on the key points from today. The rest of this book focuses on composition and writing techniques used in specific situations, so it is important that you feel confident before reading on.

Writing effective letters

Perhaps the most common form of written communication is the letter. Thank-you letters, love letters and letters to prospective employers are all examples you may be familiar with. In social writing, there are a number of conventions that encourage you to write in a certain way. The focus of this book is writing for business, and in particular writing copy that sells.

Today, you will:

- Look at both usual and unusual reasons for letter writing
- See how letter writing can build business relationships
- Consider how to balance formality with familiarity
- Practice writing some letters for your business
- Discover how email can take things further, faster

Why write a letter?

You might think that in this age of electronic communication there is little place for letter writing. However, as you will see later, email is an entirely different medium from the letter. A letter can do more than deliver a message.

A letter can:	Example:
Convey a subtle quality message	Heavyweight watermarked paper
Be clearly personal	Signed by the writer

Create impact and anticipation	Envelopes can be sealed with wax
Contain enclosures	Photographs, product samples
Provide a record of an agreement	Confirming what has been discussed in a meeting

A letter, unlike an advertisement, newsletter or brochure, is a personal communication from one individual to another. Although you will send the same letter to a number of different people, each recipient will only see one copy: it might be the only one they receive that day. Make it special enough for them to want to read, and then act on what they have read.

Drayton Bird, one of the UK's most respected direct marketers, talks about the 'three graces' of direct marketing. These define the advantages of writing a letter: it enables you to:

- Isolate someone as an individual and demonstrate your knowledge of what makes them or their situation unique
- Build a continuing relationship with someone, responding to their feedback with further communications that prove you want to meet their needs
- Test ideas, offers and concepts by writing to people and inviting them to respond. Evaluating the response to your 'call to action' enables you to see just how desirable your offer is

Reasons for writing

Before exploring the different elements of a letter and why each requires your careful attention, make a list of the reasons you might have in your business to write letters. If you think hard, you will probably find opportunities that you had not considered, which need you to create a database and record information about those you seek to influence.

Imagine that you run a restaurant in a small market town. You want to get more people using your restaurant and, more importantly, returning for a second or third meal. Some reasons to write a personal letter to your customers and prospects might be:

- To tell them about a special offer that will fill tables on traditionally quiet nights
- Invite them to special themed events, e.g. wine tasting, Christmas, Mother's Day

- To let them know about new services, e.g. children's parties in the afternoon
- To offer them an incentive to recommend a friend to try you for the first time
- You know when their birthday or wedding anniversary is and want to suggest they visit you
- They might bring business to you, e.g. funeral directors arranging a wake

The letter itself

Yesterday we considered some aspects of typography; today, we will look at the content of the letter. You probably already have a printed letterhead that provides your contact details and outlines what it is you or your organisation does. Following this, you should have:

1 *Recipient's name and address*: should be clear and correct. Avoid making mistakes with titles and honours; simply write 'John Smith'.

2 *Date*: it is always important to date your letter. This avoids confusion, particularly when you have written before.

3 *Dear*: politicians always handwrite the 'Dear Mr Smith' line. You do not need to, but choose either 'Dear Mr Smith' or 'Dear John' depending on the level of formality you feel is appropriate.

4 *Content*: makes your objective clear and also asks for some action by the reader.

5 *Sign off*: 'Yours sincerely' is always the best bet. Save less formal options, such as 'Kind Regards', for less formal communications such as email.

6 *Your name*: always type your name in full, i.e. 'Bill Jones', rather than 'W Jones'. This makes it easier for the recipient to address you personally when they reply.

If you have an unusual first name, it might be good to add a Mr, Ms, Mrs or Miss prefix to avoid embarrassment.

7 *PS*: can be irritating, but a good place to add a personal message to a mail-merged letter as you print them.

Letter-writing practice

Imagine that you are running a motor dealership and want to keep in touch with your customers. First, make a list of reasons why writing regular letters might be profitable for you.

Here are a few to get you started:

Reason	Benefit
Check that customers are happy with their new cars	• Pre-empts complaints • Collects testimonial for your advertising • Demonstrates that you care
Tell them how regular servicing reduces running costs	• Promotes your servicing workshop • Shows you can save them money

| Invite them to a new model launch | • Gets them into your showroom/new car
• Maintains personal contact
• You show them new things first |
| Congratulate their car on its imminent 3rd birthday | • Reminds them that you do MOT tests
• Means you know when car needs replacing
• Proves that you remember |

Pick one of your reasons and start writing the letter, but leave a space to add more content. Deal with layout, recipient's name, date and signing off. The content requires a little more planning.

You should now have a letter that looks good if rather meaningless; a good reminder that a letter without a clear purpose, however well presented, will go straight into the bin. Think back to Sunday and the idea of focusing on what you want the reader to know, think and do. Decide what these might be in this letter, then write the content, dealing with each in turn.

Below is an example:

Dear Shaz,

Now that you have been driving your new **Audi A4** for **three** months, I thought I should write to ask how you're finding life with your new car. It is, after all, only when you really get to know a new car that you really appreciate its finer points. Do your **children** enjoy the ride in the back?

To help me tell more people about the comfort, economy, safety and tremendous value for money that Audi deliver, I'd be grateful if you would complete and return the enclosed short questionnaire. If you return it within two weeks, as a token of our gratitude for your honest feedback, we will give you a voucher worth £20, redeemable against the cost of your car's **first** service.

I look forward to hearing from you soon.

This letter uses enough information that is personal to the reader (shown in bold type) for them to believe that they are the only recipient. This shows the value of maintaining a good customer database that contains more than just the name and address. Also included is an incentive to reply by a certain date, which will boost response: urgency always creates impact. The incentive offered will actually cost very little, particularly if the driver would not have chosen your

garage for their next service. Remember the golden rule of marketing: it is always better to sell more to existing customers than to find new customers.

Databases

You have seen from this example that the more you can tailor your letter to your reader, the more personal it will seem. This is not surprising, but consider how many letters you receive that demonstrate how little the writer has bothered to find out about you. Does anyone actually like being addressed as 'Dear Sir or Madam'?

Before reading this section, you might like to visit www.dataprotection.gov.uk to see how the legislation created in the UK to give people access to data about them might affect you. This site outlines what constitutes good practice, and compliance with it will not inhibit effective marketing in the ways encouraged by this book. You should also try some of the specialist 'contact management' software packages available. They differ from standard databases in that they can give you prompts: you can record when you next need to contact someone and why, and the software will remind you. This may seem unimportant if you only have a few customers or contacts. However, to form a close and effective relationship with your contact you need to know as much as possible about them, and you must let them know that you know.

Below are some examples of data you might choose to record and refer to:

Information	Enables you to:
Date of birth	Send a card (with product message) on their birthday Offer age related products (credit cards at 18 etc.)
Interests	Introduce contacts with shared interests Theme mailshots for groups of contacts
Company year end	Offer capital equipment at an appropriate time
Partner's name	Involve both (clearly) in the business idea suggested Invite both to events (partners often are either involved in smaller businesses or work for another you have yet to contact)
Product usage	Offer replenishment stock before need identified Develop planned (rather than emergency) maintenance

Practise writing paragraphs to go into your sales letter that contain some of this information. It will help you appreciate how valuable it is, increasing the relevance of the message and making it personal. Of course, you need to recognise that different situations demand different levels of communication 'intimacy'.

Below are two examples, one appropriate, one not:

> Dear Tom, now that you are 18, you no longer have to rely on your parents' credit cards for making those online purchases. You can apply for your own card, which means that your purchases will not appear on their statement!

> Dear Mr Jones, having reached the age of majority, you are deemed capable of managing debt and with this in mind, we are delighted to enclose for you an application form for our credit card.

If you were just 18, which do you feel would appeal more?

In writing letters to market your product or service, it is very important to pitch your language at the age and situation of the reader. The more you can use technology to create an effective and accurate record of your prospects, the more personal your letter will appear to the reader

It is also worth remembering that it really is permissible to write as you would speak. Banish phrases such as 'may I take this opportunity' and 'assuring you of our best intentions at all times': they are clichés of the worst kind and will discredit your message.

Fax

A few years ago, it was unusual to go into the office in the morning and not find an unsolicited fax lying in the tray.

This was because people recognised that faxes were cheaper and quicker to send than letters. You can use the mail-merge facility in your word processing package to personalise faxes in the same way as letters, and even program your PC to send the faxes overnight. However, faxes do not arrive in an envelope, so are never as personal as letters. What is more, most people these days have email, and so you should really leave 'mass-faxing' to those who wish to market discounted products by faxing advertisements indiscriminately.

Email

Email as a medium has revolutionised business communication. It is direct, instant, flexible and can bypass even the most diligent 'gate keeper' protecting their employer from unsolicited calls and mail. Email is also a less formal medium than a letter, and liberties can be taken that should never be considered when writing a letter.

Email writing is different from letter writing in that:

Letter	Email
Protocols such as 'dear' and 'yours sincerely' must be followed	Being recognised as a speedy, instant medium, you start with the recipient's first name and sign off with 'regards'
Follows an established flow as already described	Brevity is everything and you can 'cut to the chase' straight away

Rarely copied to others	Others involved are frequently copied in
You tell the whole story and seek a response	You tell just enough to prompt a response, then reply in a tailored way
You have to print and enclose any extras	You can attach files and hyperlink to web pages, referencing your offer

When writing an email, always remember that the recipient will probably view it on their PC, so your message will have equal weight to others in the 'in-tray'.

The ten top tips for sending business emails are:

- Keep the message short and to the point: make your objective clear
- Always seek a response: ask your recipient to 'click and reply'
- Write in the first person, e.g. 'I want to tell you about . . .'
- Avoid lurid backgrounds and 'comic' fonts (Refer back to 'Monday' for ideas)
- Always format and insert a 'signature', i.e., your name and contact details at the bottom, as people sometimes want to reply by 'phone
- Do not use the urgent 'flag' or other 'gimmicks' in Outlook. Instead, compose your 'subject' line to attract attention

- Keep subject lines to 8 words, so that they will all be visible in the 'Inbox'
- Only use symbols, e.g. (;-) or abbreviations with people you know really well
- Do not use jargon that your recipient might not understand: Say '*click here to see the relevant page of my website*' rather than '*follow the hyperlink*'
- Compress large attachments to reduce download time. Better still, ask before sending large files. (What sends quickly via 'broadband' can take hours to download on a basic home 'dial-up' account)
- Remember that many company 'firewalls' screen out messages with rude and other key words. Some seemingly innocent messages can therefore easily end up on the screen of the company's IT manager. The offending word may be 'embedded' within another (e.g. the Yorkshire town Penistone) or have two meanings ('tart' on a menu may be fine, but could be screened out as potentially sexist)

Uh - IT'S A RECIPE FOR APPLE PIE ...

There is another marketing benefit of email that is frequently overlooked. With most organisations, a visit to their website will reveal the formula by which email addresses are specified. Having identified the person you need to contact, it is often quite simple to guess at their email address. What is more, if you guess incorrectly, the mail will 'bounce' back to you, prompting you to have another try.

Summary

Today you have explored letter writing and developed some new reasons for writing letters to those you seek to influence. You will also have developed your letter-writing style and learnt how to create a logical structure. Formality versus familiarity has also been covered, although much of this is for you to decide: a young person will probably write in a more informal style than someone 30 years older. What is important is that your reader can see the real 'you' coming out of the lines on the page.

You have realised that fax has a place, but not for much longer, and that email is the business communication of the day. Email is instant, unobtrusive and interactive. What is more, it provides a 'subject line', which has the same effect as an advertising headline and should be written in the same way.

Making advertising work for you

In many ways, advertising is the most exciting form of copywriting. The space you have purchased to deliver your message is usually expensive and cannot afford to be wasted. As you do not know who will read your words, each one has to work really hard. Clarity, focus and a logical sequence that enables the reader's eye to traverse the page and get the message are essential. Even more important is the need to stimulate some response: that way, you can measure your return on investment.

Today, you will:

- Consider a range of types of advertisement
- Explore the language of advertising
- Practice writing advertising copy
- Discover how to construct effective display advertisements
- Consider unusual advertising opportunities, e.g. posters

Why do we advertise?

Advertising is used where your prospect cannot readily be identified and written to as an individual. It also has a role in building awareness and confidence in the product or service you are promoting. Awareness raising is particularly important with consumer products, where the manufacturer will advertise to create consumer desire. The retailer then supports this 'campaign' with in-store material (termed 'point-of-sale') and the design of the packaging does the rest.

However, awareness-raising advertising is usually prepared
by professional advertising agencies. This chapter will help
you prepare advertisements that you place to generate a
direct response.

Some possible advertising opportunities that you might
encounter are:

Opportunity	Suitable for:
Classifieds	Selling a second-hand car Renting a spare office Retailing firewood
Recruitment	Finding new staff
Tenders	Seeking new suppliers
Directories	Listing your product/service next to your competitors'
Exhibition catalogues	Encouraging visitors to your stand
Display advertising	Attracting new customers

You may be able to think of other advertising opportunities;
some more are explored at the end of this chapter. The
techniques that you develop with each of these types of
advertisement will help you to prepare any kind of
advertising copy.

The brief

Before you start writing, it is vital that you know the full story of what, when, who and why. If you are writing the copy for your boss or a colleague you may not automatically understand what it is that they want. Before starting to write, it is always a good idea to get a clear brief. This is what professional copywriters always do, as it avoids confusion and potentially costly mistakes.

Some questions you should always ask your client (or yourself) before planning your ad are:

What is the offer? What makes it better than the alternatives?

Who is the target audience?

Which attributes of the offer will appeal most? Is there evidence you can use?

Why should the reader do something now? Urgency is vital to success.

> When will the ad appear or be read? At Christmas?
> Morning paper, evening paper?
>
> Where will it be read? At home, at work, commuting?
>
> How do you want your reader to respond? Phone,
> email, coupon?

Only when you are confident that you have a clear brief can
you expect to write an effective advertisement.

Writing style

Advertising is a good example of a situation where 'less
equals more'. Advertising copy has to paint pictures in the
mind of the reader, but equally important is the need for
brevity. The reader must be encouraged to use their
imagination: do not try to tell them too much.

Below are some examples that show how words can paint
pictures:

What it is	How you describe it
Your wife's car, which needs replacing now a baby is on the way	*Pregnancy forces sale of treasured 1992 Fiesta*
The cat has just had kittens – again!	*Fluffy, friendly kittens seek new homes*

You need to recruit someone to clean lorries used to collect abattoir waste	*If you've got the stamina, we've got the guts!* *Determined truck cleaner needed*
You are a window cleaner	*Want a brighter outlook?* *Let me make your windows sparkle*

Note how powerful the example that uses the word guts is. This is a homonym: both meanings of the word are relevant to the line of copy, making it particularly memorable. As discussed on Sunday, homonyms, alliteration, simile and homophones are all ways of making advertising copy stand out from the page.

Now think of some advertising opportunities you might encounter and build a similar table. Include some from your home life and some that relate to work.

Let us now examine the different advertising opportunities you may encounter.

Classified ads
Many of the examples given above apply well to classified advertising. This is where your ad appears in a column, on a page, under the publisher's classification. In these situations, it is best to follow the convention used by the publication. For example, if you are selling a car, it will be listed amongst everyone else's. If they list the cars alphabetically by make, you need to start your copy with the make of car, then move into some creative text.

There are different types of classified ad:

- *Lineage*: all ads are printed in columns with each new ad starting on a separate line. The first few words are usually printed bold.

- *Semi-display*: as above but usually with a line between ads, creating a little more space and a lot more impact.

- *Display*: as above but with the words printed in a box.

- *Colour*: colour can be used usually as a tint behind the ad. This almost always costs more.

Classifieds are a good place to start writing advertising copy because they tend to be small, are often sold by the word and are very direct. These, however, are not excuses for a lack of creativity. The words need to fall into a clearly defined sequence:

1 What are you selling? Give description of the item, following the style of the publication

2 Why should I buy it? Add some further descriptive text that 'sells'

3 Where are you? If you want buyers to visit you, let them know where you are

4 How much? State the price and whether it is negotiable

5 How do I contact you? Give a phone number and an email address if possible

Now imagine that your company has just invested in some new office furniture and you want to sell the old desks. They are serviceable and clean, but rather old. Your research tells you that they are probably only worth £50 each. Your company has a van, so you could deliver them.

Below are two possible ads. Which would you be most likely to respond to?

OFFICE DESKS Clean and undamaged, choice of 10 modern double pedestal desks at our Wimbledon office. £50 + vat each. Tel: 020 8123 4567 during office hours.

OFFICE DESKS Office refurbishment makes 10 desks redundant. Perfect for your new business. £50 + vat each. Can deliver. Wimbledon. Tel: 020 8123 4567 (9–5)

The second ad contains two fewer words, but says much more. Stating the reason for the sale, 'refurbishment', suggests that the sale is not due to the desks being tatty. It also helps to tell the reader whom you think the desks will best suit; in this case, a new business for whom money is tight and appearance important.

It is now time for you to write some classified ads. Try to write, in less than 30 words, ads for some used wooden pallets, 500 rolls of parcel tape and a vacuum cleaner. Try to bear in mind the likely context within which your ad will be read.

Recruitment

Recruitment advertising is rather like the 'lonely hearts'
column. You want to find people you can work with, not just
people who can do the job. Most of the job ads you see are for
people to join 'dynamic fast growing' businesses. However,
not everyone wants to work for this type of business, and if
yours is a 'lifestyle' business, then say so. Recruitment
advertising is the home of endless, meaningless copywriting
clichés. Avoid phrases such as 'fast growing' or 'rapidly
changing', and never make a job out to be more than it really
is. People respect honesty; misrepresentation only leads to
disappointment, either at interview or, even worse, after a
few weeks in the job.

Recruitment ads tend to be either classified or display
depending on the salary offered and level of seniority. More
senior roles also tend to be advertised nationally, and lesser
roles locally.

Here are two examples of ads for an office cleaner, appearing
in a section of part-time jobs. Which appeals to you.

Cleaner required for busy restaurant. Hours flexible but must fit with opening times. 18 hours per week. £4.50 per hour. Call Luigi on 020 8789 6543

Cleaner Delight our diners by keeping our busy restaurant spotless. 18 hours a week at times to suit us both. £85 per week. Call Luigi on 020 8789 6543

Can you see how the second one is more appealing? It shows that Luigi values what his cleaner does, and is willing to negotiate on hours. The weekly pay also sounds more attractive then the hourly rate. Both ads describe the restaurant as 'busy', which is important as it reassures applicants that the job will last.

Now you can try to write some recruitment classifieds. Think of a really good job and a really awful one and write ads for both, keeping to about 30 words.

In display recruitment advertising there is a lot more scope for creativity. However, be careful, as you can make an ad so creative that the original meaning is lost. A good display recruitment ad should have:

- *Job title*: describes exactly what the job is.

- *Rewards package*: if you leave out the salary people will not apply: show a salary range.

- *What is involved*: lists the kinds of duties that need to be done. Is travel involved? Is it a customer-facing role?

- *Why you are recruiting*: is it a new job, or a vacancy created by promotion or retirement?

- *How to find out more*: encourage people to visit your website to find out all about your organisation: it is cheaper than including it in the ad. Include your logo and other relevant logos, e.g. 'Investors in People'.

- *How to apply*: do you just want people to write or email? An invitation to phone for an informal chat can be a great benefit to both parties.

- *What is special*: try to include something special that adds appeal e.g. funded training, subsidised travel, free health insurance or the fact that your organisation has won awards for employee care.

Below is an example:

SALES MANAGER – USED CARS

Basic £24,000 pa, open-ended commission structure

Do you have the enthusiasm, drive and determination to lead our team of talented car sales professionals? If so, you will relish the challenge of building our turnover and sharing our profits. This new appointment is prompted by the recent completion of a used car showroom next to the city football ground.

We can offer you a competitive package, budget responsibility and full marketing support.

For an informal chat, call our MD Steve Smith on 01234 456789 or email him on *ss@classymotors.co.uk*

Can you see how this ad is full of positive news? This is a new job, at a new showroom next door to a place where lots of used car buyers regularly congregate. There is a team to manage, a budget allocated and the package is open ended. As many potential candidates are likely to be working for local rivals, they are invited to 'phone for an informal chat. If the job was for an accountant, then it would be more appropriate to ask for written applications supported by references: you need to vary the style according to the role and organisation.

Now write a recruitment ad for your own job. When you have finished, see how far it resembles the reality of your role.

Directories
For directories, such as the *Yellow Pages*, you have to provide your copy with no knowledge of what will appear around it. Many advertisers book large, expensive ads in the hope of catching more customers' eyes. However, it is often the words or images that leap out of the page, rather than the size of the ad.

Directory ads can be very expensive and people often buy them because they feel that they should. Below are a few techniques that will make your directory ads more effective:

Feature	**Example**
Make the headline personal	*Our printer accessories last you years*
Link to your website: it will be updated more often than the directory	*Visit www.bumperdeals.co.uk for this week's special offer*

| Encourage enquiries, as well as orders (you will get more calls and more sales) | *Ring for your FREE copy of our 'guide to home improvements'* |
| Offer several ways to respond | *Ring, fax, email, write or call in . . .* |

Exhibition catalogues

Whilst you are in effect buying a directory ad and should write it accordingly, you do have the opportunity to link the ad with your stand. For example;

- 'Bring this ad to our stand and we'll give you a free cup of coffee'
- 'Ring us and quote "ABC123" and we will pack a free gift with your first order'
- Picture your stand, or the staff on it, in the ad. The curious will come and look to see if they are the same!
- 'Visit our stand, under the pink balloons, and we will give you a balloon to take home for your kids'

Display ads

These are the often large, colourful ads that combine a memorable headline, picture or pictures and some supporting text. Some of the most successful display advertising campaigns have been developed by people working within the organisation. Advertising agencies can add value but it is important to have some strong ideas of your own before delegating such an important aspect of your marketing.

We have already discussed how the eye scans a page, and you understand why most ads have a picture at the top, a headline underneath and the body-copy, i.e. descriptive text, underneath. The reply coupon, phone number, voucher etc. is usually at the bottom right, where the eye 'instinctively' ends its journey through your ad.

There are many specific books that describe, analyse and teach the art of advertising copywriting; we will just consider the basics.

Let us imagine that you have decided to place a series of display ads for your company's IT training courses. You have agreed the brief with your colleagues and want to attract 100 people to join ten half-day sessions called 'the internet for beginners'. You particularly want to attract older people. Opposite is an example of what the ad could look like.

Note how the bravery theme keeps coming up in the text, and the way the headline, body copy and picture are linked. People will phone to ask for a leaflet, providing you with the opportunity to sell them a place. The ad is also explicit in setting out the cost and what it includes. Most people will feel reassured by this: if you do not state the price they will not ring to ask, in case it is too expensive.

To reinforce your skills at writing display ads, find some in a magazine or trade journal and see how they follow the principles described in this book. Taking one that appeals to you, try to re-write it and improve it. Next, write an ad for

BE BRAVE AND HOLD THE WORLD IN YOUR HAND

Have you discovered the power of the internet? Do you shop all over the world from your living room? Are you able to keep in touch with the grandchildren using email?

Millions have already found the courage to become 'silver surfers'. Why not take the world in your hand and attend one of our half-day workshops? If we can't get you confidently online in one 3 hour session, we'll give you your money back.

Call 0800 123456 for details, or pop in to ABC Training, ABC House, Alphabet Street, Wordsville (Mon–Fri 9–5) and pick up a leaflet.

Places cost £75 including VAT, refreshments and a copy of *The internet revealed* (cover price £12.99)

your organisation in a similar style. Finally, show the work to a trusted colleague or your partner. Do they get the message you are trying to convey?

Unusual advertising
Advertising can be fun, especially if your product or service is suited for special locations. Below are a few examples to stimulate your imagination:

Location	Headline	Product
Back of a bus	*'Ever wished your car had more poke?'*	High performance cars
Above a urinal	*'Can we lend you a hand?'*	Temping agency offering factory staff
Roadside hoarding	*'No one queues on our network'*	Telecoms provider
Restaurant bill	*'Need a taxi?'*	Minicab firm
Bus (upstairs)	*'Enjoy more of a view?'*	Holidays
In a lift	*'Feeling hot?'*	Deodorant

Summary

Today you have explored advertising and gained a better understanding of how to write with the clarity and focus needed in this challenging, yet creative environment. You have practised writing copy for a variety of ads and seen that with advertising, less really can deliver more. This chapter has also enabled you to put into practice much of what has been covered in the earlier chapters, for it is in advertising that typography and photography really come into their own.

You should now feel confident to move on to consider how else you can improve your organisation's image and marketing through the expert use of your pen.

Communicating clearly with the media

People tend to believe what they are told by the media: it is more believable than advertising or direct mail. Generating effective PR is, therefore, an important skill. Today, you will develop that skill and practise the art of managing media relations: there is more to it than persuading journalists to write your story.

Today, you will:

- Understand how to build good relationships with journalists
- Discover how material is selected for publication
- Practise writing news releases
- Create and value opportunities to be asked to comment
- Recognise that bad news needs releasing as well as good

How do journalists work?

Contrary to what you might have been led to believe,
journalism today is a tough job. It is much more than a life of
leisurely writing punctuated by expensive lunches provided
by PR agencies. Harsh commercial pressures on media
owners mean that costs have been trimmed to the extent
where most journalists have little time to go out and seek
stories, but must rely on the news coming to them. Most
newspapers, for example, subscribe to 'news feed services'
such as Reuters and PA, who provide a constant flow of
national and international news accompanied by pictures.

Your opportunity is clear. In a business environment, the
newspapers, journals and magazines are generally relying on
you to tell them what is going on. However, before we
discuss techniques, it is important to underline how varied
the media is: not all types of publication come readily to
mind. Below are listed some types of publication, together
with their benefits to you as a publicist:

Media type	Benefits
Community publications, e.g. Parish Magazines	Usually produced by amateurs and desperate for material; perfect for local retail businesses
Professional network newsletters	Usually also produced by amateurs and eager to accept copy that adds to their members' professional development. You can also offer yourself as a speaker to these networks

Local weekly newspapers	Often give free editorial to advertisers, so always ask. If free circulation they often welcome product-linked competitions as these allow them to demonstrate that they have a readership
Regional dailies	Usually under severe pressure from nationals and keen to print positive local stories; reluctant to print damaging or negative stories that might jeopardise advertising revenue
Local radio/TV	Both BBC and independent stations are usually happy to publicise good stories; you may be invited for a live interview
Specialist magazines	There is a magazine for every conceivable consumer interest; check in a directory such as *Benns*. If you sell to consumers in a specialist sector, these titles can be vital
Business journals	Similar to regional newspapers
National daily newspapers	Have big editorial teams and are deluged with news releases: you need to be practised, or lucky, to get results. Be careful of damaging backfires
National Sundays	Similar to national dailies, except that they have large teams researching and writing non-news features. They frequently contract out sections to independent writers, who are easier to influence
Mass market magazines	Similar to national Sundays, but focus on their niche
National TV	Treat as you would a national Sunday

You can see that there is a complex array of media to choose from. It makes sense to target those that:

- Share your target audience in terms of interests, industry and geography
- Carry advertising from organisations in your sector, particularly your competitors
- You know your existing customers read and enjoy
- You read regularly yourself

This will give you a better chance of being heard. It is also easier to build a relationship with writers on specialist or regional titles, because you both know that there is more to be gained. National journalists, by the very nature of their publications, have to grab the story and move on; they are rarely interested in follow-on stories.

How are news releases selected for publication?

Before you write your release, you need to understand how a busy editorial office works. You can then, appreciate why it is important to work in a way that makes the journalist's life easy.

Journalists are driven by deadlines: a daily newspaper, for example, will have several deadlines a day. Features writers have much longer deadlines, and therefore work further ahead then their news colleagues.

Weekly and monthly titles will have a mix of non time-critical features and stories that are current at the time of publication. Most publications also have a constantly changing pool of 'filler' pieces that can be dropped in at the last minute if a story is stopped by the Courts or if an advertiser misses their copy deadline.

To succeed in getting your piece published, you have to present your story at the most appropriate time. For example, if you are approaching a daily paper:

Event	Procedure
Celebrity visit to your premises/ photogenic event, e.g. chimney demolition	• Send release 2 days before the event • Include biography of celeb/ information • One day before – ring to follow up • 0930 on the day – ring again
Major contract win/jobs created	• Send release straight away • Following up next day
Interesting but not time-sensitive story	• Send in with a good photo • Wait!
Disaster	• Prepare your statement and ring the editor • Listen first and be prepared to say 'I'll check that out and ring you back', and then do it!

Writing a release

There is a clearly defined sequence you must follow when putting together a news release. We will deal with each step in turn.

Photo
The most desired feature of a good press release is a professionally taken, appropriate photograph. Newspapers are always short of good shots and a photograph accompanying your release will boost your chances of exposure.

Photographs should:

- *Create a visual metaphor*: e.g. interesting shot of people with product linked to the headline of the release.

- *Avoid visual clichés*: e.g. handshakes, hands clasped together in front of trousers.

- *Not overtly promote your brand*: i.e. not look like an advertisement.

- *Catch the eye*: be innovative, yet acceptable to the paper.

A good picture is therefore the first thing you need to write your release. The picture will often give you a lead into the headline and story you want to write.

Headline
Headlines should be short (up to ten words), attention grabbing and clearly linked to your picture. Use the techniques already covered to make the line punchy and memorable. Homophones, homonyms and alliteration are particularly powerful when used in headlines.

For example:

> 'Major contract sets plane sailing' (homophone): joinery business wins big order
>
> 'Cash crisis dogs cats home' (homonym): an appeal for funds
>
> 'Mouse mat moves millions' (alliteration): mouse mat company's new product

Headlines should use the style of language that your target reader will be most comfortable with. In a trade journal, for example, your headline can be quite specific and technical, as it only needs to be understood by a knowledgeable journalist and the expert reader. In the consumer press however, jargon and acronyms, e.g. IIP, should be avoided: it is better to state the name in full, e.g. Investors in People.

Now try writing some headlines yourself for the three stories below:

Story	Photo
City mayor welcomes first 'budget airline' service to local airport	Mayor in official garb in front of 'plane, holding a £20 note and a passport
Leading research chemist becomes non-executive Director of your company	Scientist in white coat with can of your product over a Bunsen burner
Famous chat show hostess opens social housing development	Famous person hugging an old lady in the doorway of her new home

First paragraph

After the headline, this is the most important section. Many journalists will read no further and will use the content of your first paragraph and headline to create a 20–40 word caption for the picture. Others will use the same words without a picture as a 'nib': place it in a column of news snippets down one side of a page. Your first paragraph therefore has to summarise everything you want to say. Below is an example:

HANDY TO SHAKE ESSEX ENTREPRENEURS

Colchester based ABC Training will welcome business guru Charles Handy as guest speaker at their 'enterprise conference' taking place on 3rd March at 6pm. Handy will be speaking about his latest book, 'The Elephant and the Flea'. Tickets cost £25 and can be booked by ringing 01206 123456.

This paragraph contains the location, date, time, host,
speaker, ticket price and a contact number: everything that is
needed for the reader to make contact with you.

Second paragraph
This should support and expand on the first paragraph. It
may get cut or missed out altogether, so it has to really add
value. One of the best ways to do this is to include a quote.
Quotes are important because they do not get edited: they are
either reproduced in full or discarded. In the example above,
a quote by Charles Handy would almost certainly be used, a
quote by the CEO of ABC Training might be used, and one
by someone else would probably never be used. As quotes
are printed as such, it is essential to have the written
permission of the speaker to include it in your news release;
if you do not, they can sue you.

Below is a possible second paragraph for our release:

'*The similarities between Handy's book and
Colchester's business community is amazing*',
commented Bill Hook, CEO of ABC Training, '*many of
our businesses have been started by exiles from
corporate life, reinventing themselves as what Handy
would call "fleas*".'

You can see that the second paragraph consists of a quote by
the CEO. Handy, we can surmise, chose not to offer a quote
for publication. The quote reinforces the relevance of the
event in the reader's mind, linking the speaker's topic with
Colchester.

A third paragraph might contain further, supporting evidence of the significance of the event, such as government statistics on Colchester's business population and the barriers to their greater success. These could then be linked with more information about the speaker's presentation.

Lastly, a press release needs to have a clear ending – the word 'ENDS' should be written after the main text. This should be followed by information about the accompanying photo, together with contact details to enable the journalist to find out more if they wish.

Below is an example of how a release might end:

> . . . Colchester's businesses are predominantly run by men in their 40s.
>
> ENDS
>
> Picture shows, left to right: Bill Hook, CEO ABC Training; Charles Handy; Taff Dell, Founder of SX Computers, Colchester: at ABC Training's Station Road premises.
>
> For further information:
>
> Bill Hook, Tel. 01206 123456 Mob. 01712 345678
> *bill@abctraining.co.uk*

Having sent in your release, it is important to be easily contactable. Many releases are rejected because the journalist cannot get answers to questions when they need them.

Becoming a commentator

Newspapers, particularly local and regional titles, constantly seek to put a local slant on national and international stories. You can help them to achieve this and gain valuable publicity for your business at the same time. You have to:

Take action	E.g. (for accountancy firm)
Spot stories that are relevant to your organisation	*Fiasco at Tax Office as 10% of tax returns submitted on last day*
Identify your opportunity to put your own 'spin' on the story	*We are proactive and all of our clients' returns were sent in two weeks ago*
Contact relevant local/journalist	*It's as much the accountant's fault for being passive and not helping their clients meet the deadline. We do X, Y & Z and all ours were in 2 weeks ago*

| Journalist runs follow up story the next morning | You are quoted as a responsible accountant who blames less professional firms for fiasco |
| Journalist writes piece on similar subject in future | They ring you for a comment, which gets you and your firm's name in the paper |

As a good copywriter, you should be able to translate the national headlines into stories that you can submit as comments. Try to write 100 word comments that can be emialed to your local newspaper or business magazine for the examples below:

You are	National story
Shoe retailer	*Fashion shoes can deform children's feet*
Coach operator	*Tunnel work will close main rail-line for 2 weeks*
Conveyancer	*Searches failed to spot planned asylum seekers camp*
Hospital administrator	*Patient left on trolley for 24 hours in casualty*

Below is an example comment, based on the last example, to help you. Note how the quote, which will not be edited, forms the largest part of the comment.

Commenting on the saga of Jack Dawe, the pensioner left on a trolley for 24 hours at London Central Hospital, Bill Sykes, Administrator at Anytown General said, *'however busy our casualty department gets, we have the procedures in place to make sure that this could never happen here. Every patient is checked in on arrival and an automatic system of "pager-prompts" make sure that they are never overlooked, however busy we are'*. Mr Sykes went on to tell us that Anytown General regularly stages major disaster exercises which tests their system to the limits of feasibility. One of the key measures of success for these exercises is the extent to which other emergency admissions are delayed by the rush as disaster survivors are brought in.

The first part of the comment is what you might have written. The second part results from a conversation with the journalist. It is always good to have some points you want to say noted down before phoning the media.

Dealing with the unexpected

However staid your organisation, there is always the chance that you will hit the headlines. Accidents, fires, industrial tribunals, legal battles or employee misdemeanour can all attract unwelcome publicity. The worst thing to do in this situation is to say 'no comment': it looks, when printed, like an admission of failure. When such things happen, you should prepare a statement. You often see these read out by solicitors on TV news broadcasts, standing outside the Court. A statement is very different from a press release. It will often be quoted verbatim by the media and should, if the event is serious enough, be checked over by your own solicitor before distribution.

Statements are usually:

- *Factual*: explicit in the way they tell your version of the story.

- *Third person*: the organisation is 'speaking', so usually 'We believe that . . .'

- *Straight*: no humour or room for anyone to take offence.

Imagine that you are a school Headteacher and your caretaker has just been arrested for downloading indecent material onto his computer. Your statement might read:

'Mr Green is an excellent caretaker and has been with us for twenty years. The alleged offence took place when he was at home, using his own personal computer. The Governing Body has, however, decided to suspend him on full pay pending the outcome of police investigations. We hope that we will soon be able to reinstate him and wish to reassure parents that we have absolutely no evidence that his behaviour whilst at school has ever given cause for concern.'

Key points to note when writing a statement are:

- *Start with a positive*: reassures people and also shows you are unbiased.

- *Explain the facts*: in our example, the alleged offence took place at home.

- *Explain your actions*: what has been done and why?

- *Confirm your findings*: what have you found out that will reassure readers?

Before you leave this aspect of copywriting, it is worth mentioning the value of email in communicating with the media. News releases are increasingly emailed, with digital photos attached in JPEG format. This means that you can have your comment on the morning's big story in the journalist's email inbox before he arrives at work. This speed of response benefits both of you, as it helps printed media to keep up with more spontaneous media, such as radio.

Summary

Today, you have found out how journalists operate. They do a difficult job, and have to please their readers, editors, publishers and advertisers as well as you. You have also found out how a good picture can boost a news release's chances of publication.

Your copywriting skills have been developed through practising writing news releases, and you have prepared comments that you might send to gain publicity through association with existing, topical stories. Finally, you have gained an appreciation of the importance of issuing a statement, rather than remaining silent, when disaster strikes.

Preparing promotional print

Promotional print, such as brochures and websites, brings together many of the copywriting, typographical and visual skills that you have developed this week. In a smaller organisation, leaflets might be produced in-house, using 'desktop publishing' software. Large corporate brochures tend to be produced by marketing agencies, but you will still need to provide a brief. More often, a graphic designer, either freelance or with a small agency, is hired to create the visual aspects of your print and it is left to you to prepare the words.

Today, you will:

- Pick up some tips on choosing how to produce brochures
- Gain an understanding of how the print business works
- Practice writing brochure copy
- Appreciate the value of covering letters, and try writing one
- Discover how to make it easy for your prospects to respond

The basics

Producing promotional print is always a compromise. In an ideal world, you would tailor each copy to the needs and interests of the person you are sending it to, as with a sales letter. However, despite the ready availability of desktop colour printers, digital printing and colour copiers, the only way to achieve real quality is to use a professional designer and litho printer. Most promotional print needs to be professionally produced, eliminating the possibility of individual tailoring.

Below are some examples that illustrate how to select the best medium for each project:

Project	Printed solution
Invitations to a reception/ presentation	Gold-edged cards
Internal document about training options	Desktop published and photocopied
External document about training courses	Single-colour printed leaflets
Annual Report	Two-colour printed brochure
Product launch	Full-colour mailshot
Corporate brochure	Full-colour brochure

When having leaflets and brochures printed, you need to know a few facts about the printing process:

- *Number of pages*: most presses print 4 A4 pages at a time, so multiples of 4 will always be the most cost effective.

- *Paper type*: standard types of paper, whether gloss, matt or silk art paper are always far cheaper than more specialist types. It is often cheaper to use special finishes such as highlighting pictures with 'spot varnish' than to use special paper.

- *Paper weights*: measured in 'grammes per square metre' (gsm): copier is 80gsm; letterhead 90gsm; lightweight leaflet 115gsm; most brochures and leaflets 135gsm; brochure cover pages, if different from contents, 200gsm; folders and invitation cards 350gsm.

- *Quantity*: use digital printers for runs of less than 500, and 'litho' printers for runs over 500.

- *Special finishes*: 'spot varnish' is a glossy finish applied to part of the page, e.g. over pictures; lamination is the glossy or matt finish often added to covers.

- *Pictures*: never skimp on photography, or use digital images that are low resolution.

- *Providing artwork*: for all but the simplest designs, let the printer design and supply your copy as digital file for the printer to place.

Writing promotional copy

As you will rapidly discover, you can spend a lot of money on print. You must remember that brochures are often filed away and referred to weeks, months or years later. It is important, therefore, that your words work really hard and can manage on their own without you to interpret them.

Below are a few golden rules:

- Make frequent use of the words *you* and *yours*: they build the reader relationship
- Avoid writing in the third person: it is better to convey a personal message
- Talk benefits not features: focus on what is important to the reader, not you.
- Use pictures to tell the story, with captions and tables to make things clear
- Ask questions in the copy to focus the reader's thoughts

Below is an example of how you might choose to describe a public speaking training programme in a leaflet aimed at middle managers seeking to build their confidence.

Presentation skills for nervous speakers

This one-day course will help you to overcome the natural fears we all face when asked to speak to a group. Working alongside no more than nine other delegates, you will have the opportunity to discuss your concerns, then learn and practise techniques to overcome them. You will also make one short video-recorded presentation and receive individual feedback and tips on your technique.

The example specifies exactly to whom the course is aimed and implies that the provider recognises your nerves and will not take you too far out of your 'comfort zone'. A small group of like-minded people and individual feedback sound reassuring. Would you sign up for this?

Now practise describing something your organisation provides in a similar way, using a block of around 70 words. Think about what images might illustrate the benefits to which your reader will relate. Surprisingly, you will often find that the best images are not those of your product or premises: 'stock images' showing seemingly unrelated things are sometimes far more effective. For example, you might illustrate our public speaking course with a pair of nervously clenched hands, rather than an image of a confident speaker at a lectern. People buy things that relate to where they are, and promise to take them towards their goal. Showing the goal alone can make the reader feel inferior to other prospects and often inhibits response.

Benefits

It is worth pausing to consider benefits versus features. Every aspect of the offer you present in promotional print should be described in terms of the benefit it offers to the reader. People do not buy things, they buy what things will do.

Below are some examples:

Feature	Benefit
Company website	You can place your orders whenever you wish
Fleet of 10 vans	We deliver in your neighbourhood every day
Car with cruise control	Discover the joy of passing traffic cameras without worrying about your speed
First class rail tickets	Non-standard people need non-standard accommodation: buy yourself space to think
Spectacle cleaning fluid	Let people see your eyes, not greasy thumbprints

Benefits are often emotionally derived and not linked to the actual physical nature of the product. First class carriages tend to have fewer seats and thus more space, but space alone is no incentive to buy. Space to think, however, flatters the reader by suggesting that their thoughts will be valuable and worth the extra investment.

Practise writing benefit statements for the following examples:

- UHT long-life milk
- Hand-held computer
- Courses that increase your typing speed

Stopping and starting

Your reader will scan the page and only pick up some of the words. They will then, if you are lucky, go back to the interesting bits to read more. It is helpful, therefore, to have some techniques to hand that will encourage your reader to stop and think, as well as some ways to direct them towards the next section relevant to them.

A good way to get your reader to reflect on your words is to ask a rhetorical question: a question that is asked in order to make a statement and which does not expect an answer. Below is an example:

> When passing traffic speed cameras, how often do you find yourself looking at your speedo rather than the car in front? This is natural, but also rather dangerous, for in your enthusiasm to avoid a speeding fine, you run the risk of colliding with the car in front, should it stop suddenly. A good way to avoid both fines and accidents is to make sure that your new car is fitted with cruise-control.

You can also ask the reader to 'tell you' what they think. Of course in reality they cannot, but you can make them think of what they might say if they could. Building questions into your copy brings it alive and creates conversation with the reader, and conversation is always more interesting than simply listening to speech. Questions involve the reader, and involved readers stay reading.

One way to direct the reader towards the most relevant section is to produce tables, or use colour to signpost the reader through. For example:

What kind of dog do you have? If it is short haired, turn to the comb selection on the opposite page. If it has long hair, the products described below are more suitable.

The conversational, directive style will help the reader find their way about. It will save them time and, by acknowledging that dogs have both short and long hair, demonstrate an understanding of the reader's situation.

Captions
As discussed earlier, captions are important because they help the reader to understand why you have put the picture in the brochure. For example, a photo showing the view of a dashboard and car windscreen, could pose the question, *Where do you look first?* Alternatively, you could use a photo of a finger on the cruise control switch, with the caption *Cruise control is simple and safe to use.* Avoid stating the obvious, except occasionally, for example in technical brochures, where you often need to show people what the product looks like. In these cases, the caption needs to be explicit and descriptive. Sometimes, several captions are needed, each with an arrow pointing to the feature they describe.

Brochure flow
Rather like a sales letter, the information in your leaflet or brochure needs to follow a logical sequence. Unlike a sales letter, you have more space to work with and can provide a number of routes through your copy, using the techniques already described. Part of the skill of a good graphic designer is to make it easy to follow a clear, visual route through your piece of print. Below is a rough guide to how a brochure should be structured:

1 *Front cover*: instantly recognisable key benefit to reader.

2 *First section*: explains why the product or service is valuable.

3 *Middle section*: offers examples, testimonial, options.

4 *Rear section*: gives specifications if necessary.

5 *Every page*: how to find out more (why just put this at the back?).

6 *Back cover*: contact details, and possible endorsing logos (e.g. ISO9001).

The covering letter

By now, you appreciate that effective copy is personal copy, where you can create the illusion that the words have been written specifically with the individual reader in mind. By the very nature of the printing process, leaflets and brochures can be produced in vast quantities. How, then, can you personalise the message for each recipient? The answer is to write a covering letter. A number of techniques for personalising letters have already been described, such as the use of mail merge and a good database to embed personal information. When a letter introduces an enclosed piece of print, you can go a little further and really make the reader feel you are writing to them alone. Below is an example of an extract from a letter accompanying a coach holiday brochure sent to an existing customer:

You will see from page 12 that we are once more returning to Blackpool, a destination I know you have visited with us before. This time, we have included a free night-time tour to see the famous winter lights. I hope this will tempt you to travel with us again in 2004.

Linking your bookings history with a mail merge means that you can automatically adapt each letter according to the purchasing history of your customer. This, together with taking the time to hand sign each letter, really makes recipients read the brochure in which you have invested.

Think about how you could personalise the covering letters you might send, and integrate specific information that would make the letter personal. It is also important to think about how to make it easy to merge: unless you are careful, you will find that some versions of your letter look odd. It is all too easy to become careless when despatching lots of brochures and covering letters. You must remember that when the envelope is opened, the communication is very personal to the reader, and they will spot any errors you have made.

Below are a few more tips for writing covering letters:

- *Bookmarks*: when referring to a specific page (as in example above) why not insert a sticky note to mark the page? If every letter refers to the same page, the printer can insert the bookmarks for you.

- *Endorsements*: the covering letter might carry more weight if it is from someone other than you. For example, if promoting an event with a leading speaker, ask the speaker to agree to the letter going out as if written by them. This can be a powerful delegate attractant.

- *Joint letters*: professionals often collaborate to run events and campaigns, e.g. a solicitor working alongside an accountant. Prepare a special letterhead with both logos and have it signed by both participants. Unique combinations of familiar brands really catch a reader's eye.

- *Gimmicks*: in the right situation, enclosing something like a free pen or window sticker can add impact: it is better still if you can link it to the message. For example, an explosives company could enclose a balloon and a pin, to make your own big bangs!

- *Be natural*: take your product benefits to your customer: an egg producer might enclose a soft feather, or a garden centre some seeds.

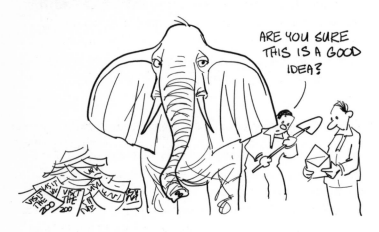

Provoking response

Of course, what makes all this effort worthwhile is the
response. You are sending out material to tempt people to
purchase, and so every effort must be made to provoke an
enquiry. Your copy needs to encourage readers to seek
further information, or indeed to place an order. Below is a
list of a few techniques to help you do this:

- *Order form*: include order forms with your brochure.
  Always send a new order form with the goods, plus an
  incentive to buy again.

- *Survey*: a simple questionnaire asking your reader's views,
  plus offering to share the findings, will encourage response
  and give you valuable feedback. Good for capital goods
  which will not be ordered 'off the page'.

- *Incentive to refer*: offer a discount on the first order if two
  additional prospects are provided for your database.
  Always use the referee's name when following up.

- *Keep writing*: follow-up letters are proven to work

- *Introduce deadlines*: early-order discounts.

- *Offer choice*: the more options you give for ordering (phone,
  fax, internet) and the longer 'opening hours' (always state
  them) the more you'll sell.

Now think about your own organisation. Make a list of the
things you want your readers to do. It might be to make an
order, book a place on a programme or simply to ask for
more information. It is always better to provide several small
steps for your prospects to follow, to make it easy for them to
move towards your desired outcome. What are the steps you

could ask your audience to take? How many are there? Write some paragraphs that seek commitment to each one. How does this compare with what you are currently doing? As you refine and test the process, you can monitor both the additional cost of more frequent communication and the return.

Summary

Today, you have gained an insight into how brochures and leaflets are produced. You know the significance of the number of pages you choose, and appreciate that the more colour you use, the higher the cost. This should get you thinking creatively about design as well as copywriting.

You have also practised writing brochure copy and have discovered the power of rhetorical questioning to make your reader stop reading and start thinking. You can then focus their attention on what will influence them most.

Distributing printed material is best done with a covering letter to enable personalisation. Although this letter needs to be written by you, you have seen that it could be printed on someone more influential's letterhead, and bear their signature.

Composing reports, proposals and presentation visuals

There are some writing opportunities that we have so far left out. There is not space today to explore every opportunity, but we can cover a few specific types of copywriting that should not be overlooked.

Today, therefore, you will:

- Practise writing proposals
- Discover how to write for Powerpoint™
- Consider the importance of effective signage
- Recognise the opportunities vehicle livery presents

Proposals

After the sales letter, the follow up brochure and a successful sales presentation, the proposal is the next piece of copywriting you need. It could be argued that all proposals are sales documents, even if only intended for your boss: you are likely to be keen to achieve the outcome you are proposing.

Remember the importance of sticking to the three key objectives when planning out your proposals: what you want your reader to know, think and do as a result of reading your words. Within the context of a proposal, it is important to be explicit. For example, if you are recommending an investment in a new, faster file server for your department, you might want the reader to:

- **Know**
  - The size of your team and how reliant they are on IT
  - The cost per minute of your team (salaries/overheads etc.) and the cash payback on investment
  - That you are working at capacity and need more staff/time

- **Think**
  - That your department is crucial to the success of the organisation
  - That increasing your efficiency will create additional, unmeasurable benefits elsewhere
  - That, otherwise, key staff might become frustrated and leave

- **Do**
  - Agree to invest £10,000 straight away in a new file server

When writing a proposal, you need to remember that it is special in that your reader has requested the information you are providing. They are interested in the topic and may well want to believe in what you propose. This highlights the other key feature of successful proposals: they are short. Information that supports your argument can always be placed at the back of the document, in an appendix, but always aim to keep the main document four pages or less.

To achieve this you can:

- *Use bullet points*: to provide succinct detail and make reading (and re-reading) easy.

- *Use footnotes*: footnotes can either expand on the point you are making or, preferably, refer the reader to an appendix.

- *Use tables*: to summarise and to provide comparative data. Graphs can be even better, but do also give the actual figures.

- *Number pages*: you can also number paragraphs, but this suggests the document is too long.

Structure

If you write a lot of proposals, you can save yourself a lot of time by sticking to a common structure. However, do avoid the temptation to create a new proposal by editing one you prepared earlier. This makes the focus of the document decay, and means that you run the risk of forgetting to delete copy that is specific to the original proposal. This is a common problem, and one that loses customers: no one wants to buy a second-hand idea.

The best method is to create 'proposal templates' that not only give you a common structure, but also a common style. Below are some possible headings:

1 *Background*: why is the proposal being written? This is a chance to reflect your version of the brief, to demonstrate that you understand it.

2 *Challenge*: two or three bullet points that summarise the need.

3 *Opportunity*: two or three bullet points that summarise your solution.

4 *Activity*: how your solution will work, step by step.

5 *Benefits*: what the activity delivers and what it is worth.

6 *Budget*: what it is all going to cost.

7 *What next*: call to action. Introduce urgency if possible.

Language

It is of course important to use language with which your reader is comfortable but do try to make frequent use of the words 'you' and 'yours', and almost always write it in the first person. This implies that you are taking responsibility and ownership. Writing in a corporate style, e.g. 'we recommend', although it suggests a degree of collaboration has taken place, is not as powerful as a personal plea.

It is now time for you to try this approach yourself. Write a proposal that recommends that your boss buys each of your team a copy of this book (in no more than 600 words). What would the business benefits be if everyone became a more effective writer?

Powerpoint

Powerpoint has made it easy for everyone to use colourful visual aids for their presentations. However, too many people simply use it to reproduce their notes on the screen. Below are six top tips for using Powerpoint:

- *Colour*: keep things simple and always put dark text on light backgrounds. Avoid strident colours and be conservative.

- *Text*: large, clear and not all capital letters.

- *Questions*: questions on the screen can focus the audience.

- *Pictures*: pictures and a few words are better than many words.

- *Animation*: special effects detract from the message: avoid them.

- *Sound/video*: sound and video clips can be powerful, but only if they are good recordings. It is better to let the speaker do the talking.

Signage

If you have a retail outlet, or simply a site with lots of people, you will appreciate the value of effective signage. At locations such as hospitals, where people may be unfamiliar with the place and also may be distressed, signing is vital. Below are some pointers to help you:

- *Clarity*: signs should be easy to read (as with Powerpoint).

- *Brevity*: use as few words as possible.

- *Sell benefits*: e.g. *free range* eggs, *great value* cars, *bargain* books: selling signs are like advertising headlines.

- *Avoid negatives*: even prohibitory signs can be positive: '*Access required 24/7*' is nicer than '*No parking*'.

Perhaps the most creative copywriting opportunity can be found on vehicles. This is because you can:

- *Use humour*: playing on your company name or product benefit, linking it to the fact that the words appear on a vehicle.

- *Use shape*: you can cheaply cover a whole vehicle with lettering.

- *Use a mirror image*: reverse words on the front of a vehicle, so that they read 'properly' in a rear view mirror.

- *Use travelling advertising*: remember that your vehicles are travelling advertisements. The technology exists to reproduce your advertising on, for instance, the back of a lorry: if you are selling to consumers, do not miss the opportunity.

Summary

What you have seen today will have made you realise that whatever you write, wherever it will be read, there are common-sense rules that apply. Once you have started, you will see countless opportunities to deliver your product, service or corporate values message to those you wish to influence. In many instances, those messages will be the same. If you are writing material for internal consumption within a large organisation, it should ideally reflect the commitments offered to customers.

As you develop your copywriting skills, you many find that you discover a passion for the power of influence that our words can wield on our behalf. Reading widely and experimenting with form, content and shape will help you to develop your skill. The real key to success is experience. The more you write, the easier it will become: practice makes perfect. Now it is down to you to seek perfection.

chartered
management
institute

inspiring leaders

The leading organisation for professional management

As the champion of management, the Chartered Management Institute shapes and supports the managers of tomorrow. By sharing intelligent insights and setting standards in management development, the Institute helps to deliver results in a dynamic world.

Setting and raising standards

The Institute is a nationally accredited organisation, responsible for setting standards in management and recognising excellence through the award of professional qualifications.

Encouraging development, improving performance

The Institute has a vast range of development programmes, qualifications, information resources and career guidance to help managers and their organisations meet new challenges in a fast-changing environment.

Shaping opinion

With in-depth research and regular policy surveys of its 91,000 individual members and 520 corporate members, the Chartered Management Institute has a deep understanding of the key issues. Its view is informed, intelligent and respected.

For more information call 01536 204222 or visit www.managers.org.uk

For information

on other

IN A `WEEK` titles

go to

www.inaweek.co.uk

Did you enjoy reading this?
Do you want more time to learn new skills?
Why not try our new Six Weeks To range:

- MARKETING EXCELLENCE:

  includes: Marketing Plans • Viral Marketing • Building a Brand • Direct Marketing • Free Publicity for Your Business • Consumer Behaviour

  isbn: 0 340 81261 3 Price £15.00

- FIND A JOB

  includes: Planning Your Career • Job Hunting • Writing Your CV
  • Succeeding at Your Interview • Tackling Interview Questions
  • Assessment Centres and Psychometric Tests

  isbn: 0 340 81259 1 Price £15.00

- STRATEGIC EXCELLENCE

  includes: Business Strategy • Staff Retention • Operations Management
  • Total Quality Management • E-Business Strategy • Business Recovery Planning

  isbn: 0 340 81260 5 Price £15.00

- PROFESSIONAL EXCELLENCE

  includes: Project Management • Negotiating • Time Management
  • Dealing with Difficult People • Presentation • Memory Techniques

  isbn: 0 340 81262 1 Price £15.00

LEARN MORE FOR LONGER WITH SIX WEEKS TO
visit us at www.inaweek.co.uk